Dental Wealth

How to Invest in a
Dental Practice
to Create Financial
Freedom

Eric J. Morin, MBA

Dental Wealth

Cover by 90-Minute Books

Distributed by Bublish, Inc.

Published in the United States of America

170711-00855-2

Paperback ISBN-13: 978-1-950282-80-7
Digital ISBN-13: 978-1-950282-79-1

Here's What's Inside...

Dental Wealth!

Congratulations for picking up this book! You've just taken the first step in your journey to creating Dental Wealth. You might just be starting to think about how to achieve wealth or you might have spent an entire career in dentistry, but still wonder why you are not financially free. In my career, I have worked with hundreds of dentists, helping them utilize their business to create a financial path to wealth. This book is an introduction to my proven process for helping dentists move their practice and wealth to the next level. My years of experience and lessons learned are ideal for helping the doctor who is looking to achieve their financial goals and impact their lives and those lives around them. Most dentists do not know how to effectively utilize their practice to achieve wealth. This is a problem that I want to help you solve.

When doctors struggle financially, they often are not sure where to turn. The most common decision is to reach out to a dental consultant or financial advisor. However, there are a few things you need to understand so that you can make the best decision for your situation. The main goal of a consultant is usually to focus on growing revenues, and the main focus of a financial advisor is to make investments outside of your practice. Realistically, a dental practice can produce between a 15% to 35% (or greater) rate of return. Since that is the case, most dentists should learn how to reinvest into their practice, not outside of, especially as that investment is considered pre-tax and the same as investing in a traditional qualified retirement plan.

True, the business consultant might grow revenues, but growth is not enough. Most individuals will spend what they make, or not know what to do with the additional revenue. My goal is to show doctors not only how to grow their practice, but also how to turn their growth into tremendous wealth.

To clarify what I mean by "wealth", it is financial control and the ability to have the life that one wants. To be clear, retirement and wealth are different concepts. While a wealthy person might retire, the goal of retirement is to grow and accumulate cash, stop working and hope you don't outlive your money. The goal of wealth is to have your income, net worth and assets increase every year, be passed on to future generations and have impact even after you have left this world.

In retirement planning, the main strategy in your working years is to save as much money as possible. This is what investment advisors refer to as the accumulation phase. Once you reach the peak retirement age (typically 65), ideally you are told you will be able to start spending that money and the main goal is to not outlive your money. Let me say that again: The main financial goal of retirement is to not outlive your money!

If you do not believe me, pull out the last financial plan an advisor gave you. In retirement, the assets (accumulation) typically goes down every single year.

The goal of creating wealth is to have your assets and income **go up** every single year. You should have the time and ability to travel and to be with the ones you love. Wealth should also be utilized to create tremendous impact. This includes impact on organizations, future generations and your community. I was recently working with a client, and his goal is to create a 35-million-dollar trust so his kids can spend their lives impacting others. Now that's what it's all about! Your assets and income should be going up every single year. That's correct, even if you stop actively practicing, your assets and income should keep increasing.

In this book, I will be discussing how to achieve this goal and create enormous wealth.

The clients who come to me range from high-end cosmetic offices (fee-for-service) to even a few low-reimbursement Medicaid offices. I am 100% confident in my process and it works every time! I am not going to tell you it's easy to create wealth, as that would be foolish. Quite the contrary; it takes hard work over a period of time. You just have to be willing to put in the time and effort, but I promise you the results are worth it and the impact you can have is unimaginable.

Many clients come to me when they are actually doing quite well and need that next level of advice. I relate it to fitness. If you are 100 pounds overweight, almost any fitness trainer can give you advice that will help you, but what if you are an ultra-marathon runner? When you become elite, it's harder to find the sophistication you need.

However, if you are struggling, this book is also for you. One of my favorite examples is a client who came to me in her late sixties and was in a difficult financial position. She had been running a small Medicaid office and had never collected more than $350,000 in a year. Within 12 months, she was not only on track for a million dollars in revenue, but she had also purchased another piece of real estate, significantly reduced her debt, and was opening a non-Medicaid location. Trust me, the same exact results can happen for you!

Congratulations again! By choosing this book, you have already taken the first step to significantly impact your financial life. I hope it inspires you to have a change in philosophy that will help you understand the power of a dental practice and how it can be used to create Ultimate Wealth!

To Your Success!

Eric J. Morin

Why the Typical Retirement Model Does Not Work

I have had the unique pleasure of sitting down with literally hundreds of dentists from all over the United States and even some dentists that practice in other countries. In my experience I will tell you that the number of dentists who have accumulated enough for so-called "retirement" is probably around five percent. In fact, the American Dental Association has compiled statistics and stated that an overwhelming number of dentists will retire with less income than they had while they were working.

Everyone wants to believe he or she will save the way they need to; however, the truth is that the majority of individuals spend what they make, while thinking, "Down the road, I will be able to retire." or "I will start saving more next month, next year," and so on.

Most individuals honestly do not understand what true accumulation looks like. For a typical dentist, it would take him or her about 30 years to save a million dollars. In retirement, there's something called a "preservation of capital" strategy. During that time, you're trying to be quite conservative. Basically, you're looking at returns of 3% or 4% because you don't want to lose your money.

However, let's assume that is not the case, that you were able to get the 7.5% that most financial advisors will tell you is possible. Once you pay taxes and fees, then you're left with around 5%. Well, at 5% of a million dollars, you will be left with $50,000 a year, or approximately $4,100 a month.

If you look at what the average dentist is spending, they could not afford to pay their current bills with $4,100. Therefore, the doctor would have to start dipping into the million dollar principal. Every month of every year, the doctor will start taking money away from that million dollars. This leads to what financial advisors call the **Death Spiral**, which happens when you have to keep utilizing your principal to keep up with a standard of living. **If I can give you one piece of great advice, it would be to not allow someone to put you into the death spiral!**

To overcome this, advisors will tell you that you don't need to worry about the death spiral, because in retirement your spending and need for income will go down. Let's first analyse that statement. Are they saying, if you work with them for 30 years, your income will go down?"

That is what you are being told. Let me ask you this question. **Do you spend the most money when you are working or when you have free time?**

If you are retired and have unlimited free time, do you think spending goes up or down? There has been a tremendous amount of research on this topic, and the truth is, spending goes up in retirement for two main reasons, free time and health care costs. Retirement can be broken down into two phases, and financial advisors will refer to these as:

Phase 1: Active Phase of Retirement

Phase 2: Passive Phase of Retirement

In the active phase of retirement, doctors want to enjoy the fruits of their labor. They want to visit their grandchildren and see the world. This is the time when you tend to spend a good amount of the capital you have accumulated.

In the passive phase, you might assume that your spending would decrease, since you would not be traveling and spending as much. However, this is typically when we see an increase in the cost of health-care. The average long-term care claim happens at the age of 81, and if you look at the rising cost of healthcare, a claim 20 years from now could literally cost you millions of dollars. In fact, the cost of long-term care is so expensive, they decided not to put it into the Affordable Care Act when it was passed, and there are only 2 companies left in the U.S., as of this publication, writing Long-Term Care Policies. The claims were so high that most companies pulled out of the market.

You deserve a better way! The good news is that there is a better way. It's to create wealth verses trying to retire. We need our assets and income to increase every year so that we can live the lives we deserve and impact our families and communities, not burden them.

The goal of retirement is to avoid outliving your money, but you're being put into a model that doesn't offer enough money to get where you need to financially. Most people aren't accumulating. Even if they were accumulating, people don't understand the amount they truly would have to accumulate in a typical retirement model to have what they want.

For example, a dentist who owns a "million-dollar practice" should take home an annual income between $150,000 and $300,000. To maintain this level of income in retirement, you would need to accumulate between **three to six million dollars.** Doctors need to have multiple assets that allow them to maintain an income over the rest of their lives.

So let's agree, the standard retirement model does not work or is unlikely to work for the vast majority of dentists. It also does not allow you to increase your standard of living and have the same income you had while you were working. Let's also agree that you have the ability to make a tremendous financial impact in your life and in the lives of those around you. You should have more options, more quality of life, not less. I would even go as far as saying you have an obligation to create wealth. If you have the ability to use your talents to impact thousands of lives, your family and future generations, but you don't, that is arguably unfortunate.

To start this wealth conversation I want dentists to understand the true value of a dental practice. Corporations are coming in at a record pace right now, and venture capitalists are coming in as well because they understand a dental practice can yield them somewhere between a 15% to 30% rate of return with a very limited amount of risk. In fact, the risk of a dental office going under is approximately one percent.

What I want to do is help dentists realize the value in their practice and that by investing back into that practice, and using what comes out of it, they can create amazing wealth. This will allow your assets and income to go up every year, without taking money outside of your practice and investing it somewhere else.

There are times for placing money into retirement accounts. I'm certainly not saying that you should not put money into retirement accounts, but I want to get doctors away from thinking about the traditional retirement paradigm. For instance, I started working with one doctor who wanted about $10,000 -15,000 a month as income for the rest of his life. One of the reasons he ended up with me is because his financial advisor said, "That would be no problem. All you'd have to do is put away $100,000 a year for the next 20 years."

First of all, how many doctors are putting away $100,000 a year? There are very few. Even then, he wanted to retire within 10 years, not 20 years. We were able to use other assets to help him reach his goal. For example, I asked him, "Who owns this building?" He said, "I don't know." And I said, "Let's find out. Let's find out who owns this building." When we did, the person offered to sell him the building; interestingly, the mortgage payment on the building was the same amount as his rent, and we could get that building paid off within ten years. Even if he sells the practice, that building will pay him approximately $10,500 a month in passive cash flow before we even talk about the dental practice or retirement accounts. Building a wealth plan is about understanding that we need to create wealth by utilizing the assets dentists already have or can acquire easily.

When most dentists come to me at an older age, they are most often not happy with the progress they are making with their wealth. Often times, in someone's later working years they may feel defeated. Just recently, a doctor came to see me in tears. She said, "I just don't feel like I'm where I'm supposed to be. At this point in life, I should have more accumulation." (Because financial advisors will scare the heck out of you, telling you if you haven't accumulated, you will end up being destitute.) "I'm 51 years old. I feel like I'm never going to be able to retire."

We started working together, and took some money out of her brokerage account and moved it over to pay off her mortgage.

With just that one move, she went from tears of sadness to tears of happiness. She said, "I've been waiting for the day when I can pay off my mortgage."

She received pushback from her investment advisor because that's how he makes his money, but let me ask you a question, "Do wealthy people buy high, or do they sell high?" You're supposed to sell high. During the time of that meeting the Dow Jones Industrial Average was literally at its all-time high. Why would we not take some money and move it over to pay off her mortgage? We also worked through the tax implications of that decision, but it's decisions like that, made now and in the next five years, that will let her completely pay off her home and building and have zero debt. Now that she's not laying out money for debt payments, she will have a stream of income from this building, and she still has her practice. Without any additional accumulation, we just had to make a few moves to (literally) free up eight thousand dollars a month.

Many advisors will recommend that you not pay off your home. To be completely honest, I would run from anyone giving you that advice and wonder if they had your true best interests in mind. After assisting hundreds and hundreds of dentists create wealth and reduce debt, I have never met somebody, in all the years I've been doing this, who said, "Man, I wish I hadn't paid off my home. The tax breaks were great on my mortgage," or, "I probably missed out on the market." No one has ever said that. The people who pay off their homes come to me and say, "It's one of the greatest, freeing decisions I have ever made." In fact, we can grow a practice while reducing debt at the same time, and that is why my average client can pay off their home in 3-5 years.

When we focus on building wealth and stop focusing on retirement, amazing things can happen for you, your practice and your family.

To learn more visit:

Dentalwealthcoach.com

Understanding What Wealth Truly Is

Let's look at what wealth truly is. Honestly, wealth is control; it's having the time and money to do the things you want to do. If you don't have a mortgage, if you're not surrounded by debt, if you have multiple streams of income, if you can practice when you want and you have the financial means to impact those around you – then you are wealthy.

One of the clients I work with just took her family to Europe for two weeks. She is a dentist, and her practice never shut down the entire time she was away. She made just as much while she was gone as she would have made if she had been practicing. She has complete control of her time and the financial resources to go where she chooses. Isn't that wealth? She didn't lose any money being away. She has control of her calendar and her time.

Even a teacher can be wealthy. We have the idea in our minds that, "Wealth is all about having millions and millions and millions of dollars." The truth is, to be wealthy, you need control of your time and money. Wealth does not necessarily equate to masses amounts of accumulation. Wealth is truly the ability to come and go as you want, having the ability to impact the people in your life and having the ability to make the decisions you want..

One of the wealthiest, happiest couples I've ever met in my entire life never made more than $30,000 on their W-2 income. When I sat down with them, they had accumulated over $30 million. During my first meeting with this couple my office was located in a very exclusive area of town. It seemed like most the people that came to me looked like they had a lot of money, as they were driving expensive cars and had enormous homes. However, they had very limited net-worth.

When I looked at the financials for this couple and saw $30 million plus, at first I thought it was a typo. I looked at their W-2 and said, "This can't be right. What am I missing here?" I asked them how they had done it. They explained to me that once they had paid off their home, they sold it, but they didn't upgrade their standard of living. They bought a condo. They had a real estate approach, but they always kept living within their means. With this couple, I remember that he was getting a job bagging groceries, and she was getting a job at an ice cream parlor just for fun; they were flirting, laughing and enjoying life together. It was great. Because they had truly created wealth, they didn't have to work. They were living the life they wanted. They weren't stressed out about accumulation and what the market was doing.

What ends up happening is that we get caught up in accumulation; we're inundated with commercials telling us we haven't accumulated enough, or "You'll never be happy unless you have 10 or 20 million dollars." The truth is that wealth is the day when you can come and go as you want and do not have to worry about money anymore. That moment is different for everyone. It really, truly depends on who you talk to, but I will say that wealth is having control of time and money. If you can walk away from work, in a sense, you're technically retired. I have clients in their 30's that don't have to work another day. Wealth can happen literally at any age! It does not need to wait until age 65.

To learn how you can create wealth as soon as possible visit:

Dentalwealthcoach.com

Let's look at Warren Buffet for a minute. He is the epitome of wealth. He is one of the richest men in the world. Does he have to work? Yes and no. Financially speaking, he doesn't have to work. He has enough accumulation but if he left Berkshire Hathaway, if he walked away, what would happen to the company? In a sense, he's technically still working but yet, he is completely wealthy. We've been taught this paradigm in our country that if you work really, really hard and accumulate as much as possible, then you get to retire. Retirement is that special day when you can sit in the reclining chair, usually at the age of

65, and you get to wait out your days. How great does this sound?

The purpose of life is not inaction. Wealthy individuals get to relax, but instead of counting pennies and hoping not to outlive their money they get to have impact and their assets and income continue to go up year after year.

One of first places we start to build wealth is to assist dentists to get out of debt. You should be able to grow a practice significantly and reduce debt at the same time. I show all the clients I work with how to do this. As I stated earlier, my average client pays off his or her home within 3 – 5 years and pays off a multi-million dollar building within 7 years. How do I do this? By showing dentists how to invest and utilize their current assets to have a multiplier effect.

When I say the word "invest," depending on what we need to accomplish, the money might go into dental equipment, an associate, building, or another business. When doctors sit down with me or my team, they assume we have a cookie-cutter way to do this, but every meeting we have with a doctor is different. One of the things I do that is different than most advisors, is just ask,

"What do you want?"

It's interesting what happens. People in the financial world sit down, and they have their pre-conceived notion or definition of wealth, but I always start with what people want in their lives. What does that look like?

Everybody has a different idea of what he or she wants, and that's why I know that not everybody wants five locations. Some dentists only want one. Some people want a five-million-dollar practice. Some people want a $500,000 practice, but even that has nothing to do with wealth. I start people off in a process by simply asking questions:

- What do you want?
- What do you want to drive?
- Where do you want to go on vacation?
- Where do you want to live?
- What do you want life to look like?
- Who do you want to impact?

Let me take a moment and touch on the last point first. In a conversation with a doctor, I asked him, "If you were to pass on, who would you want to have impacted?" He said, "Nobody." That is **not** someone I would want to work with.

"The whole purpose of creating wealth is to impact people. Why create wealth and not have an impact?"

I can assist anyone to become as wealthy as they want, but I want them to have an impact.

Creating wealth starts with understanding of what you want. Believe it or not, sometimes this is the most difficult question to answer. As you're reading this, take a moment and ask yourself:

- What is it that you truly want for your life?
- What do you want to do that you can't do today?
- Who do you want to impact?
- What do you want for your family?

I encourage you to ask and answer these questions with your spouse. When I meet with doctors, I ask them to bring their spouse so that I can make sure both people are on the same page. Recently, I had a doctor bring his spouse to a meeting and the spouse was dreading it. She was rarely included in meetings and when she was, she found them to be quite boring.

I focused the entire meeting on her, and her main goal was to pay off the house in six years. The dentist had a million reasons why he wanted to pay off other things first. Not only did I show them how to pay it off in six years, by the time the meeting was over, we were able to pay it off in 18 months. She was extremely excited, they were finally on the same page and she now wanted to support him in other financial goals he was trying to get accomplished.

The exciting part to this meeting was, we were able to pay off their home before growing the practice by even one dollar. You can imagine where my process will have this couple in just a few years. You need to have someone who has the knowledge base and acumen to look at all of your assets simultaneously.

Another example of creating wealth was when I consulted with a 71-year-old doctor. He started working with me because his financial advisor had just told him, "Look, you'll never retire. You're too old. You owe too much. You don't have enough accumulated." The doctor had about $850,000 sitting in a retirement account, but he was also paying $9,000 a month on his building mortgage.

So I asked him, "How much would it take you to live?" Even though his financial advisor just said, "You will spend the rest of your life working, and there's no way you could ever get out of this debt," all we did was simply take some money out of his retirement account. That's right; I took it out of the retirement account (even though he and the advisor felt like that was security), and we paid off the building. The payment on the building was $9,000 a month.

Paying off the building gave him an extra $9,000 a month. His practice started paying rent to him of $9,000 a month rather than the mortgage company. Then he sold the practice as he wanted to do. By the time he was done with the structuring of the real estate, and the sale of his practice, he ended up having an income stream of about $15,000 a month. He literally was able to "retire" overnight. The same guy was told months before "retirement" could never happen.

This is why I do not support the typical retirement model. No one even looked at the fact that he had a building that could be paid off.

The advisor only gets paid for the money sitting in the investment accounts, even though that's not what is best for the doctor. For the financial advisor, there was no monetary incentive to suggest restructuring the real estate. Therefore, a financial advisor often won't make such a recommendation either due to a lack of understanding or a lack of monetary incentive.

The financial world has a major bias built into it. We all have to pay our bills; I get it. But we all have a natural bias. I always tell clients, "This is my bias. If I get you to where you want financially, (1) you'll impact as many people as possible, and (2) you'll continue to work with me. I lay that out in all of my meetings. I just want you to know what my bias is. I'm not trying to get you to buy something or sell you anything you don't need. I'm not trying to sell you any investment products. I'm here to help you get to ultimate wealth utilizing your practice."

To learn more about our process reach out to me at:

Dentalwealthcoach.com

Active and Passive Cash Flow

Let's analyze the common path for a dentist. Typically a dentist graduates from dental school and then becomes an associate. After two or three years, the associate is in his or her early thirties. In dental school, this doctor was told that owning a practice is the key to creating enormous wealth. They were also led to believe they would have the ability to be in control and choose the hours they would like to work. After taking on a significant amount of debt to buy a dental practice, the doctor gets married, starts having kids, and begins to accumulate a substantial amount of personal debt. Once dentists are in that situation, they need more and more revenue. As they build more income, their expenses increase: it's the fancier car, nicer home, bigger country club and so forth. The practice which was supposed to give them financial control and freedom is doing the opposite. In order to make money, they must work even harder.

The more revenue the practice generates, the faster it disappears. What often happens is the doctor lives off of their income instead of the revenue being generated from their assets. It is imperative that you understand the importance of creating passive cash flow. The practice revenues should not be used to provide your income. On the contrary, the revenues should be used to buy assets which in turn, create income.

The good news is that you already have one of the best places in America in which to invest – a dental practice. As I will show you later, investing in a dental practice has an incredible return. You can take that money and put it into other investments that provide passive cash flow, such as:

1. Your personal residence
2. Commercial real estate
3. Brokerage accounts
4. Qualified accounts
5. Other businesses and opportunities

Your personal residence does not provide income, but I will tell you this is one of the largest hurdles to creating individual wealth. Wealthy people do not have home mortgages!

I want to help doctors understand that the goal is not to continue making more income. If income is your only goal, you will just end up spending it. I was working with one doctor who was literally spending $193,000 a month on personal expenses. He told himself this extravagant cost was due to the fact that he lived in Connecticut, and Connecticut is just "different from everywhere else." We all justify things like that. What can be done with $193,000 a month is almost incomprehensible, yet he was still living paycheck to paycheck. The truth is, the more money you make the more money you will end up spending.

My job is to show you how to transfer that money from your hands and allocate it in a way that will generate tremendous amounts of wealth and income. If I can do that, then I know I can get you where you want to be. If you are looking to retire, then I can get you there quicker; I can also make you wealthy in your thirties or forties. Following this plan will give you the autonomy to work when and how you want to work. For example, one of the happiest dentists I work with is 83 years old. He is passionate about dentistry and he loves what he does, but he doesn't have to work. That's wealth – because he doesn't have to be there. He is able to come and go as he pleases, works on larger dental cases because he enjoys them and celebrates victories with his team.

Overall, the idea is to put more and more money into passive income sources, which is why I get doctors to start thinking about passive cash flow first. For example, **I can show how it is possible to invest in a single operatory and pay off a million-dollar building in six years.** Yes, I can take one operatory and pay off a million-dollar building in six years.

What would happen if I bought two operatories? Measuring the return on investment and allocating it immediately will ensure the money is not spent. Whether it is marketing, equipment, or growing teams, I can teach doctors how to allocate their money in resourceful ways. Believe it or not, you can experience significant practice growth and pay off debt at the same time.

To find out how to grow your practice and reduce both business and personal debt at the same time reach out to me at:

Dentalwealthcoach.com

How to Reinvest Back into Your Practice

As I said earlier, a dental practice is an amazing place to invest and create wealth. As stated in the previous chapter, you can grow your practice and decrease debt at the same time . But what does that look like?

Investing in Equipment:

Let's assume you purchase a new operatory. Maximum production for an operatory is around $40,000 a month. Imagine that we are only bringing in about half of that revenue – approximately $20,000 a month. When I say producing, I mean collecting. As an MBA, what matters to me is actual revenue coming into the business.

With an investment such as this, you are truly only taking on additional variable costs. Therefore, an additional dental chair can give you a 50% rate of return. You can take that 50% rate of return, which should be about $10,000 a month, and allocate it towards paying down debt. Let's assume that the operatory costs me $60,000 and I borrowed the money. With my $10,000 a month of additional revenue, I could pay off the operatory within 6 months and then I would have created an additional $10,000 a month in revenue. **Let's do the math: You borrowed the money. Therefore, it did not cost you anything other than the small**

amount of interest paid over 6 months. In turn, you created as much passive cash flow as a retirement account worth over 2 million dollars!

Now, let's assume we have a million-dollar building. If we applied the $10,000 to the building, we could pay it off in approximately 6 years!

In this example, the practice is growing and we are paying off a significant amount of debt at the same time. Are you starting to see the financial power of a dental practice and why it is such and amazing place to invest?

What would happen if we made these types of decisions together over the next 10 years? You can only imagine where you would be financially.

Contact me at dentalwealthcoach.com to discuss your goals.

Now that we have excess cash, we can also fund retirement accounts. In fact, now we have a different problem – determining where to allocate all the cash. It's hard for most people to imagine, but one of my clients' biggest problems is that they don't know where to put all the money. I know that sounds silly, but it's true. These are the kind of problems you want, rather than simply hoping you don't outlive your money. I want you to increase the practice growth, reduce debt, take the difference, and then invest it into other assets, which will provide additional income.

Investing in Marketing:

Let's say that you have $100,000 in net income. If you were to put $40,000 into a 401(k), it would reduce your business taxable income to $60,000. This means the financial advisor and the tax accountant are both happy. You've also accumulated savings and reduced your tax liability at the same time.

Now, let's say we look at investing in the practice again. I've talked about equipment, but this time we are going to invest in marketing the practice.

First, I need to help doctors understand a few marketing terms, such as "acquisition cost" and "average revenue per new patient". Doctors need to know how much it is costing them to get a new patient through the door and how much that patient is worth to them.

As a side note, most dentists don't have control of these numbers. Why? Simply stated, they are meeting production rather than running the business. Dentists are truly at a disadvantage, as they are often the business owners *and* main producer. However, I teach all doctors to understand Key Performance Indicators (KPI's), which can help you meet your objectives and assess the success of your practice.

Referring back to our marketing example, let's assume your acquisition cost (i.e., the cost to get a new patient) is about $115, which is typical in dentistry. (When we work together, I will show you how to calculate this number.) Let's also assume your average revenue per new patient is approximately $1,700, which is also typical of general practitioners in the United States.

If I take $40,000 and put that into marketing, and it costs me $115 per new patient, that works out to 348 new patients. If I take 348 new patients, and multiply that number by $1,700, that gives me $591,600 in additional revenue. If I assume a 30% profit margin, I would have an additional income of $177,480 after one year. If I invest in my 401(k) and use the Rule of 72, I can determine how many years it will take my money to double. (To obtain this number, take 72 and divide it by the rate of return.). Due to fluctuations in the stock market, most investment advisors will tell you it takes about ten years for money to double.

So, that means in ten years if we invest in our 401(k) with a single investment of $40,000, we'd have $80,000 after ten years. If we invest in the marketing of our practice, after year one, we'd have $177,480. Between this example and the operatory example, we literally just **increased your income by over $250,000** annually and we haven't even gotten started yet! Now you're starting to see how to build significant wealth!

This is the significance of going through my process and allowing me and my team to help you become an excellent business owner and a generator of wealth and impact.

Why hasn't anyone shown you this math before? Honestly, most individuals are only trained in one area. Also, many advisors have a bias towards the products they sell.

For example, let's take a look at what a traditional consultant does. Generally, while they may initiate processes that help the practice grow, it usually doesn't turn into wealth. Why? Individuals tend to spend what they make. Financial advisors also lack in this area, because they are not trained on investing inside your practice. Even if they were, they have no financial incentive to assist you. What about banks? Typically, they do not encourage you to pay off debt aggressively because they have no financial incentive to do so.

Certainly, I'm not saying that financial advisors, bankers, or consultants don't want dentists to be successful; however, when you start looking at it, nobody is showing doctors how to thrive as business owners and turn their income into wealth. My approach is different because I don't sell any investment products and I'm not biased.

I show doctors how to invest back into their practice to create wealth and reduce debt. I want to help doctors understand the numbers of their practice and how to create wealth. Simply stated, that is my bias.

Investing in Your Team:

One of the greatest investments you can make in a business is your team. When I sit down with doctors, I show them how to develop key metrics for each person on their team. Unfortunately, there are many individuals in the marketplace who show you how to pay your team members the least amount possible.

If we are going to create wealth, we need dependable, trustworthy people who are passionate about your business. They understand your mission and vision, and they know what is in it for them. These individuals attract more people like them. In order to be successful, you want to create a high-performing, growth-oriented team that adheres to rigorous standards. This means creating a team in which people are paid for the value they provide.

If you underpay people, you might be better off in the short run. However, I can promise you that eventually, it will cost you much more than you think you're saving.

I believe your TEAM is the backbone of your business and should be treated as such.

If you want to invest in your team and move them to the next level, I would suggest:

1.) **Determining a strong vision**: Most doctors do not have a clear vision for their practice. If your team member is not invested in your business, the only way you can compete is compensation – and someone else can always pay more.

2.) Communicating your vision: Make your team a part of the conversation. Demonstrate what running a successful practice means to you. In return, ask for their input and respect their opinions.

3.) Allowing them to see what is in it for them: Find out what your team members want. This is one of the keys to building wealth. After all, if you help others get what they want, they will return the favor.

Do you want to learn about additional avenues to invest in your practice strategically? Reach out to me today at:

Dentalwealthcoach.com

The Impact of Wealth on Your Life, Family, and Legacy

When there is true wealth in someone's life, it creates a substantial impact. This topic is very near and dear to my heart. About three years ago, one of my favorite clients was kicked out of his dental partnership, as the older partners felt he was too ambitious. He asked, "Eric, what am I going to do?" I replied, "It's the best thing that has ever happened to you."

He ended up buying a practice which had never collected more than $900,000 in 30 years. During his first year, it collected $2.6 million.

Fast-forward a few years, he recently broke down on the side of the road, right by a dealership. He was able to walk in and buy a brand new truck in cash! This same individual is now working with me to create a $30 million trust for his kids so they can spend their entire adult life impacting others. Currently, he has a nine-year-old, a seven-year-old, and a six-year-old. His goal is to spend the rest of his career creating an irrevocable trust, which his kids (as the trustees) will be able to manage, give money away, and make an impact on the world around them. Imagine that! He went from frustration and uncertainty to making a substantial contribution in a very short amount of time.

How did all of this come to fruition? If we go backward in this story, it started from a conversation we had years before. I was on the west coast speaking to approximately three hundred doctors. He had texted me that morning to ask if we could have breakfast. "I'd love to share my plan with you," he said. He and I had been working together for about a year or two since starting his new practice.

Over breakfast, he explained all of the gains he had experienced personally: he bought a building, a piece of land, paid off a quarter of a million dollars in student loan debt, plus bought a new truck in cash!

After he shared his successes, I finally asked him, "Where's the impact and generosity?" He replied, "What do you mean?" I asked, "What are you giving back?" He answered, "I don't know what you mean. I can't afford to give back right now." I said, "If you can't give ten cents out of a dollar, you won't give ten million out of a hundred million. Here's the problem, "you have the ability to impact many people, and I would love to see you do that."

I could see him starting to rethink our conversation. He asked to meet me the next morning. The next morning, we sat down and he showed me his generosity plan. Sure enough, that's what he's living now: generously.

When you look at the effects of wealth on your life and on your family's legacy, creating wealth has the ability to impact others. When you increase your assets every year, your income rises. When you start getting out of the retirement mind-set and into a wealth mind-set, you can impact as many lives as you dream possible. Look at individuals like Bill Gates or Warren Buffet. They are spending their entire fortunes giving back to other people.

The truth is, wealthy people impact other individuals. I always tell my clients, "The first group of people you should impact is your family." Having wealth – without being stressed out over debt and all of life's little problems – allows you to have the life you want for your family. First, we impact our family, and then, we can impact our team.

Recently, I was asking a doctor about her vision (which I cover further in the next chapter) for her practice. She said, "Well, Eric, I'm not sure. What do you mean?"

I asked her, "Where is this practice going in the next five or ten years? If you don't know where you're going, you won't get there." Together, we worked on creating a vision. Next, I asked, "Tell me about your dental assistant."

She said, "Well, my dental assistant is a divorced mom of two kids."

I said, "Okay, if she helps you get what you want, what does she get out of it?"

She replied, "I don't know."

I said, "Then why is she here?

If she won't accomplish any of her goals, she's just here for the pay. The problem with that, is that somebody can always pay her more. As you grow this practice, you can impact her life, right? Does she understand that helping you grow this practice will impact her life and her kids' lives?" Right then, it was clear. You have this amazing tool in your hands as a business owner, specifically as a dental practice owner, to truly have an impact on many lives around you.

Many organizations want to tell you to increase your profit by decreasing your employees' wages. These ideas, like so many others, are nonsense. Many consultants will tell you to create an incentive plan that is tied to production, I will tell you that this is a huge mistake. Study after study will prove that is not the number one reason individuals come to work. If you make work all about compensation, your team will too. They will care more about how things affect them and less on impact and proper care of patients. Hire great people, pay them what they are worth, treat them well and they will take care of your patients. This will produce all the financial results and the impact you were hoping to gain with the incentive plan.

Wealth leads to impact. Why? The more wealth the practice accumulates, the more you can contribute to the community. You can achieve this by making smart decisions and reducing the debt on the practice. Who can you impact? This is about utilizing your dental practice to give wealth to your team. In turn, your team will be able to impact their families, and together, you can go out and impact other people in your community.

That's the kind of life you want to have. Simply hoping that you don't outlast your retirement fund is not a very glamorous way to live.

I don't want on my headstone: "He didn't outlive his money."

You can approach life in one of two ways. The first is ego-centric. It's all about you and what you can have. The second is about helping as many people as possible. As Zig Ziglar once said, "If you want to get as wealthy as you want to be, you help as many other people get as wealthy as they want."

I believe in the philosophy of helping. If you help people get what they want – whether these are patients, employees, or people at your church – they will fight for your dreams. You won't have a problem with them working late hours; you won't have a problem with them coming in on Saturdays.

If you help people, they'll help you. To do this, you have to relieve some of the stress. By making great financial decisions, you will be in the position to impact as many people as possible. It starts with getting rid of this retirement model mentality, and then moving over to a wealth process based on an understanding of passive cash flow. By doing this, you can make decisions that intentionally create wealth, which you can use to impact others. It's that simple!

Start your path to wealth creation today at:

Dentalwealthcoach.com

Importance of Vision in Your Practice

When I talk about creating a vision for your practice, it needs to be solid. One of the common mistakes people make is lumping their vision in with their core values and mission statement. As we know, this usually ends up shoved into a binder and placed on a bookshelf, only to be reviewed occasionally.

If you want to create a tremendous amount of wealth, you need a solid vision.

Vision is the single most important financial tool in your practice. It will change and transform your business, your financial life, your marriage, and everything else.

Sometimes I tell this story to clients: I was sitting down with a gentleman who had just sold a 30 million-dollar business. I asked him, "Now that you've sold this 30 million-dollar business, what do you want your life to look like in five years? Be specific. What will you drive? Where will your kids go to school? What will your vacation look like?" Suddenly I realized: I had never asked myself that same question.

I went home, and I got laser-focused. I asked myself, "Hey, what do I want my life to look like in terms of health, of family, of finances?" I just laid out everything. I started eliminating everything in my life that wouldn't get me there and started adding things that did. I created a five-year vision. **Within 15 months, every single item on my list got check-marked.** This is the power of vision.

Understanding your vision and sharing it with your team will help you obtain the financial things you want. It will get you to wealth, to where you want your practice to go. You have to envision it first, and you have to know where you're going. Believe it or not, the biggest struggle that I have with dentists is not financial. That part is easy to me. The hard part is trying to get doctors to truly figure out what they want in this world; an ironclad understanding.

One group of doctors, who had come up from Florida with a partnership, told me, "We heard you are the guy who can take us to a hundred million dollar practice." I definitely could. At the time, they had nine locations. I looked at all of them and asked, "Why do you want a hundred million dollar business?" No one ever asked them what their why was. It took almost four hours to figure out their vision and what they truly wanted. The financial part is easy – growing is simply statistics. Vision is typically harder to determine; it takes time and conversation.

By the time they were done, they wanted one location with 24 operatories. Sometimes people start to get caught in ego and outside influences. They lose sight of their original goals, that is, if they had original goals from the beginning.

From a financial process perspective, I start from this point:

"Tell me exactly what you want this practice and your life to look like."

Once they tell me, I ask, "Why do you want it to look like that?" We walk through a process until I know exactly why they want and why they are doing it.

Once they have an iron-clad vision, I tell them to share it with their team. I want each person on the team to know what that vision is about.

When I sit down with my team, we start with vision almost <u>every day</u>. We have large white boards where we post our visions. We have a ten-year, five-year, three-year, one-year, and quarterly vision for our company and so should you.

Once you get your team focused on the vision for your practice and how it will impact them, they will work extremely hard to take care of your patients. Your team will come in early, stay late and do anything needed. This is when the magic happens!

Let us assist you in creating a solid Vision to build your practice on:

Dentalwealthcoach.com

You Get What You Measure

One of my number one rules: You get what you measure. Many consulting and accounting firms will tell you to focus on profit as your main key performance indicator. The problem with just measuring profit is that you get what you measure. If you're measuring profit, you'll get profit; however, there is always a cost. While measuring one thing, there is always something else you're not measuring. In any organization, you want different people measuring different KPI's.

Let's compare two different dental practices:

Practice A is mostly focused on profit margin and has been persuaded that profitability is the key determinant of a successful practice. Due to this fact it does not focus on growth and is unwilling to invest additional revenue (as that would reduce its profit margin), it sees little to no growth. However, the doctor feels good due to the profit margin. It has an annual revenue of $800,000 and a profit margin of 30%.

Practice B is focused on growing the practice. The doctor knows this investment will allow him or her to scale the business, increase net worth, and actually have the ability to provide a much better quality of life, as it can bring in other producers and pay for the best systems to be implemented. Practice B has a profit margin of only 25%, but annual revenues of $1,500,000.

Although Practice A has a better profit margin, Practice B makes more money and allows the ability to bring on an associate. Practice B allows for margin of time and money and increases wealth.

Which Practice would you prefer?

Pratice A:
800,000 x 30% profit margin =
$240,000

Pratice B:
1,500,000 x 25% profit margin =
$375,000

It's important to note that although Practice B has a lower profit margin, it actually yields significantly more profit in the long-run.

I am certainly not suggesting that profit does not matter. I just want you to understand that you get what you measure and be careful measuring too far in one direction. As in this example, you need to focus both on growth **AND** profit. Accountants tend to get doctors too focused on profit, but there are many other areas to measure.

Also, what is your high profitability costing you? Maybe you have high profit, but your team is underpaid and morale is terribly low. You might have high profit, but your lobby looks like something from the 1980's and your office is not referable, so that would cost you new patients. I could give you example after example, but as you can see, it is important to measure different areas.

On the other side, it seems at the date of this publication, many doctors are in growth mode. All they want to do is have multiple locations and giant amounts of growth. However, they are so far in debt and cash flow is so tight that one hiccup in the market could cause this practice to be in an extremely bad situation.

Just because a bank will lend you the money does not mean that the project is a good idea. All we have to do is look back at the mortgage crisis of 2007 and 2008 to see this play out. Yet, here we are again with individuals taking out giant loans with limited cash flow.

The number one need of any business is access to capital!

Remember, wealth is having the time and money to do the things you want. If you grow just to grow and don't monitor cash, you will have neither. If you do not pay attention to cash flow, you will have a much larger cash-eating machine. One day you will wake up and your company will be three times larger than but you will have three times the amount of stress. You may be busier, but you are still making the same amount of money.

So, what is the perfect balance? It's honestly less about balance and more about system. In an organization, you ideally want to have different people measuring different things. In your office, who is measuring new patients? If you're not measuring new patients, you're probably not getting new patients. Who is measuring referrals? Who is measuring team morale? Who is measuring patient satisfaction? If you are not measuring those things, you will not achieve them.

At Tower Leadership, one of the things we do for our clients is implement leadership teams. Doing so allows you to have different team members in your organization measuring different things. Your team will be able to work together and review key metrics and projects. If this is something you need to develop in your practice,

I would encourage you to contact me at

Dentalwealthcoach.com

Let's step away from business for a moment and look at your personal life. The fitness industry is a billion-dollar industry. However, I can give you the number one way to lose weight. Step on the scale every single morning. That's right, step on the scale every day without exception. There have been books covering this very topic, and many statistical studies performed. When you watch your weight every morning, it will encourage you to make different eating decisions. Those choices will cause you to lose weight. As you lose weight, you will have momentum, and as you have momentum you will be even more inclined to make better decisions. Is it that simple? Yes, it's that simple. **You get what you measure.**

You might be asking, "What does this have to do with wealth?"

Everything.

Consider your bank account. How often do you look at its balance or your credit card balances? What if I told you that you will have more money simply by checking your financial accounts every single morning? How is this possible? You will be more cautious of what you're doing. You will notice transactions and think, "Do we need to buy that? Did we mean to do that?" There is a direct correlation between what you measure and the results you achieve.

If you want to create a tremendous amount of success and wealth in this world, you need to start measuring! You also need a leadership team for your business, as you must have different team members measuring different things. You need a scorecard which contains the key metrics you should be reviewing. The doctor who tries to take on everything after being in the chair all day will not be able to consistently review these areas, and should not try. It just will not happen!

Measurement is the Key to Wealth

Once you start measuring, it will allow you to grow your business the way you desire. You will be able to maximize both growth and profitability.

You will be able to properly use debt, properly use equity, create systems, and measure the right things. You will know what to measure, and you will achieve your desired results. Best of all, **you're not responsible for measuring everything. Your team will be there to help you with that.** This is a key component of wealth.

I can turn around revenues dramatically for organizations and have done so many times. The first thing I want to know is what they are measuring. Almost every time, they are not measuring at all, and don't have the proper systems to do so. As soon as someone says, "Referrals are down," I ask, "Are you talking about that daily? Are you measuring it? When was the last time you tracked it?" When the answer is "no" or "I don't know", I know that this is why they probably aren't getting the results they are looking for: they have a systems problem.

Recently, I had a doctor tell me, "I'm panicking because our new patient numbers are down." I went to her office, and said, "Show me where your new patients are," and she showed me. I said, "Okay, let's look at last year's numbers." She showed me the last year. Then I said, "Can you show me the year before? Actually, while we're doing this, let's just look at two more years." By gathering this information, interestingly enough, this office was on pace for what they had been doing for the last five years. She was feeling panicked and had an overreaction because she had not been measuring. Once we identified that the new patient numbers weren't the actual problem, it allowed us to go back and focus on potential changes that would assist.

When we dissected the issue, the problem was that patients on the books weren't keeping their appointments. They had a high cancellation rate that wasn't been measured daily. One team member said, "It's because our old patients aren't showing up anymore."

I said, "Well, let's measure it." When we started measuring, we found that wasn't the case at all either. The actual problem was the clinic had a tremendous amount of cancellations, due to a poor cancellation policy. On top of that, they were not confirming appointments consistently. The problem had nothing to do with new patients; it was about keeping the patients they already had on the books. Increasing new patients is important, but because they were not measuring the problem, they did not understand how to fix it.

We want to hire people who are in a position to measure. In a dental practice, the doctor should present himself or herself as the CEO of the practice. A CEO sits down with his or her leadership team once a week and reviews the numbers. For our company, every single Tuesday, we go through the same process. We shut down everything from email to cell phones, and we measure for two hours. Then, we update our scorecard, review our measurements, and talk about how to improve numbers and issues. When we stay on this process, guess what goes up? **Everything!** Your organization can do the same thing whether you have 2 team members or 122.

Doctors are mainly told to focus on production and expenses. Therefore, they are often unsure about what to measure. Believe it or not, one of the most important things to measure is income. As a matter of fact, I would challenge any reader to note exactly how much they made last year–not what you tax return says, but the true amount of income you made last year. Most people need an accountant to help them with this number but isn't it important to know how much you made? When I coach someone, I want to identify what the doctor *truly* made so we can impact this number.

Why am I spending so much time in this area? This is truly the key to wealth. As I have stated, we need to know what to measure and we need to be careful of where we are getting that advice.

Let me give an example of what I mean, explain why it's important, and tell you why you need different advice. In the dental profession, it's assumed that the ideal team expense should be between 25 and 30 percent of total revenues. (This includes things like uniforms, payroll, payroll taxes, extra bonuses, etc.)

So, if the team expense is 36%, **what do you do?** Many people's natural response, especially those in the accounting field, is to recommend that someone be cut since payroll is too high. However, let's look at the same problem a little differently. From a business management standpoint, we would say that revenue needs to increase by 6% because business is focused on growth and profitability. That is typically a very simple thing to do. If you start letting people go to hit profitability numbers, what does that do to morale, or your ability to provide exceptional experience and patient care? You get what you measure!

Are you measuring your investments for growing your brand?

There are many ways to grow your brand. It needs to start internally. I go in depth on this topic with clients. Rest assured, you need to be measuring marketing. Oftentimes, if a practice is not growing, the marketing budget is less than one percent. That's pretty interesting!

Here is a good question, do you know how much it's costing you to acquire a new patient? This is a powerful number to know. What if your patient acquisition cost was approximately $115 (hint: if you're marketing properly, it should be close to this). Let's also assume your average revenue per new patient was approximately $1,500. (It should actually be higher for the vast majority reading this book.) Would you spend $115? The answer is yes, over and over again! You think corporations study patient acquisition cost?

You get what you measure!

The best practices measure. If you want to create the wealth you have always wanted, you have to start investing and measuring where it counts. I would recommend you visit **dentalwealthcoach.com** so that we can assist you. This will help you achieve the growth and profitability your practice deserves.

What if you knew the proper metrics to measure? To find out what they are reach out to us at:

Dentalwealthcoach.com

How to Utilize a Dental Practice to Create Ultimate Wealth

If this sounds like something you would be interested in creating for your practice, we can help. Many individuals attend a full-day consultation with me, typically along with their spouse. We collect as much data as we can, and then analyze. We start the day asking the doctor, "What is it you want?" That's why I want the spouse there, especially when I start going through ways to allocate capital to create wealth and reduce debt. Every time a spouse isn't present, within 20 minutes the doctor says, "Oh my gosh, I wish my spouse was here!"

Ideally, we spend the whole day creating a step-by-step plan. That plan is honestly a way to get the business where you want it to be, as well as a step-by-step personal strategy. We work on incorporating everything into one comprehensive financial plan. For instance, to meet someone's goals and reduce their debt, I might say, "We need to grow your business another $350,000 this year. To do that, we would need to invest in this area, that area, etc.

A client recently told me, "You know what I love about you, Eric? You give me the next step." I have found that giving someone the next 10 steps is much less overwhelming than giving them the next 100.

This came from years and years of working with hundreds of dentists, building their wealth, and helping their businesses. One analogy I often use when working with someone's finances is picturing trying to move a large granite ball. We've all felt that place where we literally feel like we are getting crushed. This is the place in which we feel like the weight of the world is on our shoulders.

All I have to do is get the granite ball rolling.

Do you know how hard it is to stop a giant granite ball? Once we get it moving, and we start getting all the debt paid off, suddenly there is $2,000 extra, $3,000 extra, $5,000 extra. It is like a freight train and it is unstoppable. Once I get the systems in place, there is nothing to stop you. The doctor who is building a 30 million-dollar trust is a great example because you have to figure out where to put all his money. Even though, at the beginning of the process, you feel like you're getting crushed, at the end, there is an amazing place where you have to figure out a different problem.

In most cases, I do not believe the process should start with one-on-one coaching. If you want to enjoy tremendous results, the first thing I need to do is teach you all the things about wealth and business that no one has ever taught you.

This starts with a complimentary consultation to create a customized solution for you.

Schedule your complimentary, 15-minute consulting call by visiting:

www.Dentalwealthcoach.com

I am committed to helping you achieve the life and practice you have always dreamed but it starts with making a commitment and scheduling your phone call. Our team is extremely talented and ready to take care of you however time slots are limited. I guarantee we can help you leverage your practice to create the financial life you have always wanted.

Thank you for taking the time to read this book. We look forward to serving you and assisting you create Ultimate Wealth!